Frank Lloyd Wright in a portrait probably taken when he was in his fifties. *(Photo: De Longe Studio, Madison, Wis. Courtesy the State Historical Society of Wisconsin).*

Frank Lloyd Wright

ARCHITECTURE AND NATURE

by

Donald Hoffmann

WITH 160 ILLUSTRATIONS

DOVER PUBLICATIONS, INC.
New York

Ideas can be, and are, cosmopolitan, but not style,
which has a soil, a sky, and sun all its own.
—Chateaubriand

Buildings, too, are children of Earth and Sun.
—Frank Lloyd Wright

With the exception of the frontispiece portrait, all photographs are by the author.

Published in Canada by General Publishing Company, Ltd., 30 Lesmill Road, Don Mills, Toronto, Ontario.
Published in the United Kingdom by Constable and Company, Ltd.

Frank Lloyd Wright: Architecture and Nature is a new work, first published by Dover Publications, Inc., in 1986.

Book design by Carol Belanger Grafton

Manufactured in the United States of America
Dover Publications, Inc., 31 East 2nd Street, Mineola, N.Y. 11501

Library of Congress Cataloging in Publication Data

Hoffmann, Donald.
    Frank Lloyd Wright, architecture and nature.

    Bibliography: p.
    1. Wright, Frank Lloyd, 1867–1959—Contributions in organic architecture. 2. Prairie school (Architecture) I. Title.
NA737.W7H58   1986   720'.92'4   85-29264
ISBN 0-486-25098-9

PREFACE

Nature must have meant more to Frank Lloyd Wright than we shall ever know. What I attempt here is a reasonably succinct account of the many ways in which nature inspired his principles and thus suffused every important aspect of his architecture. My method is that of epitome, which comes so well recommended by the intense discipline of his design. Where creative effort is involved, he liked to say, there are no trivial circumstances. So the visual details and the occasional references to particular buildings are expected to serve as demonstrations, the characteristic part being asked to speak for the whole and the instance for the class. Most of the illustrations will readily suggest other points and will accord just as well with other sections of the text, which I take as fair proof that Wright's principles not only were drawn from the same primary source but were, indeed, richly integrated. If, finally, this study should seem elementary, then it will have served my purpose.

D. H.

CONTENTS

Frank Lloyd Wright

ARCHITECTURE AND NATURE

1. Taliesin, near Spring Green, Wisconsin.

2. Looking south from Taliesin.

NATURE, THE NOBLE ENVIRONMENT

Frank Lloyd Wright intended his buildings to be at home in nature. The ground was more important, he said, than anything man would make out of it or put upon it. Nature came first and would last longest. Intimacy with nature would always be the great friendship. "The very simplicity and nakedness of man's life in the primitive ages," Thoreau had written, "imply this advantage at least, that they left him still but a sojourner in nature." America was born into a truly noble nature-environment. Nature offered the ideal environment for independence and seclusion. A building would perform its highest function in relation to the life within it and the efflorescence of nature outside it.

3. Wright's studio and home, Oak Park, Illinois.

Wright conceived his home in Wisconsin as a natural house in love with the ground [Fig. 1]. He faced its main living spaces toward the valley his ancestors had farmed [2]. In earlier years, he had built his home in the village of Oak Park, at the edge of Chicago; its site, he recalled, was a tangled wood of trees and shrubs and vines. Later, he had added a studio. Although it opened onto a busy street, he liked to imagine it as embraced entirely by nature [3]. Such drawings fascinated the young architect Richard Neutra, in Vienna, and led him to think of Wright's houses as all being far away in free nature, not in residential districts [4]. Wright preferred the natural site. He said that a city man who moved to the country usually spent too much on his house and too little for his ground. Wright rejected

4. The Cheney house, Oak Park, Illinois.

5. The Kaufmann weekend house, Fallingwater, near Mill Run, Pennsylvania.

the materialism that regarded nature merely as the land that men could not turn to profit, and thus set aside for public parks the most picturesque hills and valleys because they were presumed useless for either farming or house building. He imagined instead an architecture in league with the stones of the field. He persuaded a client to build her California house not on the treeless site she had already bought, but in a nearby ravine, where he saw two great eucalyptus trees. He planned a magnificent resort for a desert place in Arizona, and in a dense forest of Pennsylvania he built a weekend house above a waterfall [5].

Because the materials of architecture are largely inert, Wright wanted nature to surround his buildings with all the signs of change that speak more directly of life. Nature furnished the only grace notes for buildings limited by modest budgets. An architect should always take the landscape to be part of his province [6]. Civilization and its incursions had only made nature more precious. Wright looked to every tree with reverence. Behind the Winslow house he planned a carriage house so that a tree could rise from the stable yard and pierce its eaves. When he designed a covered passage between his own home and studio, in Oak Park, he made the roof accommodate the trunks of an old willow. To spare a tree in front of the Tomek house, he devised a detour in the long concrete flower bed. He made two concrete trellis beams curve around trees at the rear wall of the house above the waterfall, where he also changed the structure of the west bedroom terrace to allow three young trees to grow through the floor of paving stones.

When nature was not much in evidence, Wright often turned a building inward: Unity Temple, the Larkin Building and the S. C. Johnson & Son Administration Building are all examples. When a building was confined by its site, as with the Dana house or the Robie house, he often intensified its ornament to make up for the lack of natural efflorescence. His buildings were meant to rest easy with the earth and to bear an intimate relation to the life of plants [7, 8]. They were meant to bring a new order into the landscape and a new clarity to every vista. Nature and architecture: each was to be happier for the other.

6. Fields at Taliesin.

7. Grapevines at Wingspread, north of Racine, Wisconsin.

8. Hollyhock House, Hollywood, Los Angeles, California.

Where architecture met nature, Wright chose not to blur the line or plane. True friendship asked no compromise. Wright favored a strong baseline: the foundation expressed as a substantial preparation or water table for the building above it [9]. Ruskin had written that the way a building came to the ground, and its weight upon the earth, ought to be made apparent. "The foundation is to the wall what the paw is to an animal," he wrote. "It is a long foot, wider than the wall, on which the wall is to stand, and which keeps it from settling into the ground. It is most necessary that this great element of security should be visible to the eye, and therefore made a part of the structure above ground."

Wright thought that a building should serve as a foil to nature, and nature should serve a building as ornament [10]. Plants looked more lovely when presented from within the clear geometric shapes of a building and its extensions, the flower boxes, trellises, walled gardens, walks and curbs. They might be taken aboard as though the first-class passengers on a splendid ship [11]. The building, in turn, might be pushed far into its site [12]. Even

9. The Dana house, Springfield, Illinois.

11. The Robie house, Chicago, Illinois.

10. The Hills house, Oak Park, Illinois.

12. The Tomek house, Riverside, Illinois.

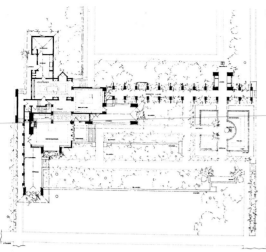

13. Plan of the W. E. Martin house, Oak Park, Illinois.

a compact or vertically disposed building could gather in the landscape through porches, arbors, flower beds, ponds and fountains [13]. Some of Wright's plans structured the landscape to correspond with the shapes of the rooms, corridors, entrances; even with the rhythm of a ribbed ceiling [14].

His flower urns grew more abstract as they began to serve as if sacred vessels, to bear offerings in place of the prairie flowers which had vanished during the years when he was a child [15–17]. Finally, he elevated the urns to form finials on the pylons that stopped short of supporting anything more than the urns themselves [18]. Thus he ornamented the absence of closed corners and simultaneously celebrated the concomitant cantilevers of the roofs: two of his greatest accomplishments, both metaphors of freedom in nature.

15. Flower urn at Wright's home, Oak Park, Illinois.

14. Plan of the Ullman house project, Oak Park, Illinois.

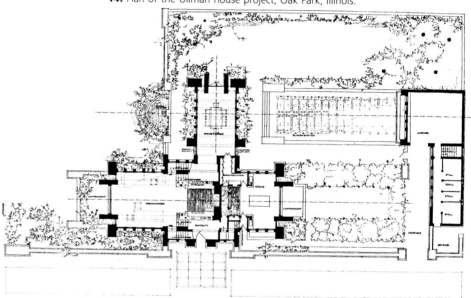

16. Flower urn at Wright's studio, Oak Park, Illinois.

17. Flower urn at the Adams house, Oak Park, Illinois.

18. The Tomek house, Riverside, Illinois.

NATURAL CYCLES

Wright conceived a building with great feeling for the primary forces of nature, gravity and the sun. Life depends on the sun and it bends soon to gravity, returning finally to the earth [19]. Gravity helps shape the form of all but the least of natural organisms. "The tree under its burden of leaves or fruit," wrote D'Arcy Thompson, "has changed its every curve and outline since its boughs were bare, and a mantle of snow will alter its configuration again." Whenever possible, Wright oriented a building to the south and slightly east, for the best light of day. He liked to adorn a building with the spilling, trailing plants that at once expressed the force of gravity and the endless cycle of life and death [20, 21]. When photographs of his buildings lacked sufficient evidence of such plantings, he felt obliged to ink them in; and in perspective drawings he often added small rugs draped over the parapets to perform the same expressive role. (Indoors, he placed scarves on the tables and animal skins loosely on the seats.) The entire form of a building might be conceived to accentuate the weight of its mass [22]. Just as a tiny root from the seed of a tree would bend toward the ground under gravity, to enter the soil and establish again a fixed point of growth, a natural and virile architecture was to bear a vital relation to the earth.

19. Wild wheat.

20. The Ingalls house, River Forest, Illinois.

21. The Coonley house, Riverside, Illinois.

22. The Westcott house, Springfield, Ohio.

23. Evening on the Iowa prairie.

NATURE'S REPOSE

When men traveled by foot or by horse, they knew the landscape intimately; it was part of their everyday life and struggle. The first and greatest of Wright's intuitions of the landscape came when he grasped the nature of the vanishing prairie and saw that it had a poetry all its own. He thought that his buildings ought to respond to its peculiar character. Later, he understood that other landscapes, anywhere, might well inspire very different patterns of design. With those two steps he set his imagination free for the rest of his life.

Most of the prairie is sloped and softly rounded, not flat, and its peaceful and expansive beauty comes from the open relation between land and sky, and from the extreme breadth of both [23, 24]. The lakes look much the same [25]. Illinois lay at the junction of timberland and prairie, as Lincoln

24. Summer sky, southern Wisconsin.

remarked; and so did southern Wisconsin. Wright spent the best months of his youth in the valley of the Wisconsin River, where the flood plain is wide and sandy and the hills above are stratified [26]. In tributary creeks the massive rock structure slumbers fully exposed [27]. The virgin prairie reached toward the horizon without any trees; later, lone sentinels grew in magnificent outline upon the horizon. From the shape of an elm tree, Wright took inspiration for the first of his buildings to speak clearly of the prairie, the Winslow house. Jens Jensen, his friend, said elms were characteristic of the low and wet places of the prairie, and signified domesticity. In the first extensive and accurate exposition of Wright's work, Robert C. Spencer, jr., another of his friends, wrote that nature had spent years in building the elm by the Winslow house, and the house conveyed the same impression as that conveyed by the elm; thus the house seemed to have as much right to its place as the tree.

Windmills, too, stood as sentinels on the prairie. Hamlin Garland thought their sails looked like the petals of prairie flowers. Wright designed for his aunts a most peculiar windmill that he became very fond of; he shaped its tower as a lozenge embraced by an octagon and named it

25. Morning over Lake Michigan, north of Chicago.

26. Taliesin.

27. Mill Creek, near Taliesin.

"Romeo and Juliet." The idea probably came instead from the top of an ordinary windmill as seen in perspective, its vane pointed like a wedge into the wheel; Wright was alert to such unexpected and energetic relations of form. He also learned much from barns, the true cathedrals of the prairie [28]. Barns answered the horizon with their immense roofs, and people on the prairie knew, if only in their bones, that when living quarters first were separated from shelters for animals and fodder, in bygone times, barns served as models for houses. In choosing Oak Park for his first home, Wright recalled, he was attracted not by the rows of Queen Anne houses but by a lingering barn; the barn, he said, at least was honestly picturesque. In an early and unrealized project for a site at the edge of the Illinois prairie, Wright designed a most handsome barn, much more accomplished than his plan for the house; and it was no accident when he advanced much further creatively in the stables for the Winslow house than in the house itself. Many years later, the barns he built at Taliesin told how much the common buildings of the prairie had meant to his architecture [29, 30]. Wright never really needed the little Froebel kindergarten toys for which his mother was so eager to claim credit; cribs, sheds, silos, windmills and barns were all strong and simple geometric shapes, and farmhouses and their dependencies composed casual but wonderful ensembles of dominant and subordinate masses, much like those he was to pursue at a more intense level of integration.

Wright saw the prairie swiftly changing, its grasses and wildflowers sacrificed to a farmland more fertile than the world had ever seen. Thoreau already had warned that the improvements of the ages had but little influence on the essential laws of man's existence; yet Thoreau's retreat to the forest, to reconstruct a solitary frontier life leisurely spent in nature worship, was a pale response by comparison to Wright's creation of an architecture of nature metaphor and high abstraction. Ruskin had come closer, by declaring that the abstract and awesome power of architecture had to do with broad and substantial wall surfaces that caught the sunlight and recalled to the mind "the joy that it has in contemplating the flatness and sweep of great plains and broad seas." Emerson said that in every landscape the point of astonishment occurred at the meeting of sky and earth. Spencer noted as early as 1900 that Wright's architecture bore an evident love for the horizontal. Wright himself, to introduce his drawings for a typical house in a prairie town, published in 1901, wrote that the exterior recognized the influence of the prairie, was firmly and broadly associated with the site and accentuated its quiet level. That same year, Jens Jensen chose prairie flowers in his landscaping of a country estate at Lake Geneva, Wisconsin. Many years later, he said that the message of the prairie had long appealed to him and he had tried to understand its force and enchantment. Jensen kept true to native plants and used them to create stratified or terraced massings which he intended as allusions to the natural transition from a mysterious woodland to the quiet prairie. His plantings stepped down from large trees (oaks, maples, elms, ashes) to smaller trees (crabapples, hawthorns, plums, cherries, dogwoods) and to flowers and grassy meadows. Wright found in Jensen a kindred soul who nevertheless imitated only the superficial aspects of the prairie.

28. Transept barn, Missouri.

Some of Wright's buildings were blocky, particularly if constrained by a small site and budget; and because of his fresh feeling for the horizontal, his more expansive buildings gained a more characteristic expression. He divided a building mass into three vividly stated strata. The ground story, of mostly unbroken wall surfaces, expressed the weight of the building and gave it its grip upon the earth; it also brought the basement up from the

29. Farm buildings at Taliesin.

damp soil and into daylight, where it could stand as a strong podium. The principal story met the outdoors through long stretches of casement windows or glass doors and provided the building with an abundance of light and air. It looked comparatively weightless. The third level addressed one more great requirement: shelter. Its radically extended roofs played with gravity by seeming to float above the open story below and expressed the basic ambivalence of the prairie, a space strong and free, but so vulnerable to extremes of heat and cold, to raging fires, to winter storms and spring tornados.

Every swift and clean stroke of the horizontal stood for values that Wright cherished. A building in love with the earth became a natural companion to the horizon. It brought life closer to the ground and into a more intimate scale. Every window and door, every molding and ceiling and

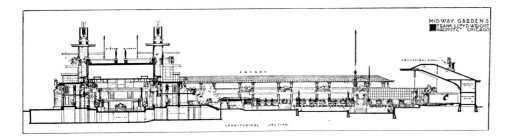

30. Silhouettes of the Robie house *(top)* and the Dana house *(middle)*; longitudinal section of the Midway Gardens *(bottom)*.

measure of height, looked more human and friendly. The new sense of scale brought a new sense of spaciousness and a special attention to vistas, indoors and out. It brought a sense of enlarged freedom and a new awareness of the depth of a life at home in nature. Horizontal lines and planes expressed the new feeling for speed, yet spoke just as well of ancient and natural patterns of streamlining and flight. All these values came together in a rare kind of repose, not merely rest, but the tranquil cadence that can occur when each part finds its right place, in equilibrium with gravity and in an abstract equivalence with the landscape.

LESSER RHYTHMS OF NATURE

Wright saw that nature possessed great powers of rhetoric. Nature rarely said something and at the same time tried to take it back, he observed. There were many patterns of horizontals that reinforced the spirit of the prairie horizon—in the rock strata, the limbs of white pines, the bark of birch trees, even in the parallel veins of the prairie grasses and of the cereals planted in their place [31–34]. When settlers came, their marks on the land often followed suit: railroad tracks from town to town, long roads

31. Rock strata, northern Illinois.

32. Pine grove, southern Wisconsin.

33. Birch tree, near Taliesin.

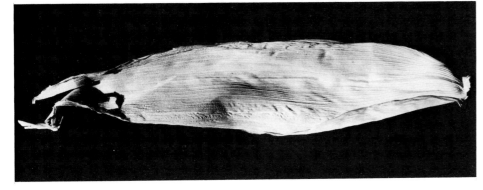

34. Leaf from a corn husk.

along straight section lines, fences that followed the roads, rows of crops and the furrows from which they sprang. Such steps from the horizon down to a more gentle scale seemed full of hints for a natural architecture. Moreover, horizontal patterns came naturally enough on the drafting board from the architect's basic tool, the T square.

Ruskin said there were three great divisions to a wall: the foundation, or base; the body, or "veil"; and the coping, or cornice. He said they ought to grow from each other like the root, stalk and bell of a flower. Wright enhanced the horizontal sweep of his walls by expressing their foundations and copings as long ledges. In the terrace parapet at the Bradley house he used lapped boards to form a miniature roof that imitated the main gable roofs of the house [35]. Sometimes he gathered copings and roofs together into clusters of horizontals [36]. For summer cabins on the lakes, he favored board-and-batten walls as a strong horizontal pattern. He used brick in a similar way in the walls of the Heurtley house [37]. More often, he specified that the mortar beds between courses of brick be raked for a horizontal emphasis, while the vertical joints were cleverly suppressed by being brought flush, their cement being colored the same hue as the brick. In the interior brick walls of the Imperial Hotel, the Martin house and the Allen house, he accented the mortar beds by having them rubbed with gold leaf;

35. Terrace wall of the Bradley house, Kankakee, Illinois.

36. Corner of the Bach house, Chicago, Illinois.

37. South wall of the Heurtley house, Oak Park, Illinois.

on some inside walls of the Dana house, he attached long stained-wood strips equal in height to one course of brick. Charles E. White, jr., while working in the Oak Park studio, noted that Wright enjoyed vaulted spaces but was distressed by the tympanums of the end walls. Wright's struggle to assert the horizontal at all costs was already apparent in the playroom mural of his home; its stratified clouds culminated in a genie with stiffened wings that cut straight through the circular enframement. When he was faced with a semicircle again in the dining room of the Dana house, he imposed a strong lintel that nearly destroyed it [38].

Ruskin noted a certain deception in Gothic architecture when its shafts and ribs resembled stems and branches and suggested a fibrous structure reaching upward. In fact, he said, the great weight of a ceiling was bearing downward. Wright effectively turned the Gothic on end. His horizontal rhythms told the truth of things by expressing the repose of masses in harmony with gravity and the landscape; his architecture spoke of life here and now, not the kingdom of a Christian heaven.

38. Dining-room lunette in the Dana house, Springfield, Illinois.

NATURE AND THE CANTILEVER

The horizontals of nature in the most dynamic relation to gravity are cantilevers. Flowers blossom as cantilevers from their stems; the wings of birds and insects, and the winged seeds of certain trees are all cantilevers meant to serve flight, the most free of all spatial events. There are cantilevers in rock ledges, such as those that helped inspire the house on Bear Run [39].

40. Shelf fungus, northern Illinois.

39. Rock ledges on Bear Run, near Fallingwater.

41. Lamp in the playroom of Wright's home, Oak Park, Illinois.

42. Master-bedroom porch at Wingspread, north of Racine, Wisconsin.

43. Unity Temple, Oak Park, Illinois.

Strange forest plants attach themselves to trees, take on the look of bark and flourish as cantilevers [40]. Yet it was from the branches of trees that Wright learned the most, as when he cantilevered the lamps in the Oak Park playroom [41]. Or he might cantilever a porch as though it were a new limb [42]. He cantilevered roofs in the spirit of sheltering boughs [43]. He imagined concrete columns as analogues of great trees that formed a forest cover, and he conceived skyscrapers with broadly cantilevered floors. A cantilever often served as a lintel that pushed far past its usual place to free a room from the traditional and confining shape. Steel and reinforced concrete, Wright said, were good encouragements to cantilever construction; but he also designed cantilevers in wood and even in stone and brick. Raked mortar beds gave masonry walls a cantilever expression, particularly at the corners. Wright believed the cantilever to be the most romantic of all possibilities in structure, and he made the cantilever his main instrument for asserting a new freedom in architecture.

IN AXIS TO GRAVITY

Plants that grow in axis to gravity constitute an essential part of nature's pattern. Without the play of vertical against horizontal, there can be no experience of three-dimensional space. Wright could see that prairie grasses and wildflowers, the plants in ponds and the kernels on an ear of corn, all formed ranks of staccato counterpoint to the breadth of the land [44–47]. He created similar patterns of rhythmic verticals to reinforce the horizontal drama of his buildings. These patterns took the place of the arcades, aisles and ranges of columns that Ruskin had found so important in establishing the power and sublimity of architecture. Sometimes the patterns, although abstract, were explicit in their imitation of nature's verticals, as in Hollyhock House [48]. The concrete mullions of Unity Temple were conceived in the same spirit, and the playful finials of the Midway Gardens were like the tall stalks of robust volunteer plants. For the Century of Progress exposition, held in Chicago in 1933–34, Wright suggested the possibility of a pontoon structure with thin tubes or "reeds" clustered to support a vast, webbed roof. The piers of his project for the Masieri Memorial in Venice would have

45. Prairie pond.

46. Roadside grass, Spring Green, Wisconsin.

44. Cottonwood sapling.

47. Indian corn.

Louis Sullivan said an architect was a poet who used materials, not words. Ruskin had written of "the nature of material." Wright grew to believe that materials were gifts from nature to human sensibilities, which themselves were gifts of nature. He wanted to "make friends with matter," as Emerson phrased it, to penetrate the character of each material and identify its essence. Through an intense sympathy with the nature of matter, he hoped, man could triumph over the superstition that separated him from its spirit. If architecture returned to a primitive sympathy for matter, it could expand and elevate the discourse between nature and man's use of its materials. Then the materials chosen for a building would go far toward suggesting its appropriate mass, outlines and proportions. When its strengths were understood and its limitations accepted, a material proved friendly, as if in gratitude for the recognition of its individuality. The architect who revealed the poetic nature of his materials offered an equivalence to the ever fresh and various textures of nature [52, 53].

52. Bark of an American elm tree, Missouri.

53. Morning glories, northern Illinois.

54. Stone wall at Taliesin.

55. Cypress siding of Wingspread, north of Racine, Wisconsin.

56. Iron-spot brick in a wall of the Robie house, Chicago, Illinois.

57. Wall of Wright's home, Oak Park, Illinois.

58. Unity Temple, Oak Park, Illinois.

The vivid expression of any material gave it an inherently ornamental value, Wright thought, and that stood him on firmer ground than either Ruskin or Viollet-le-Duc, the one having pronounced the most beautiful things in the world to be the most useless; the other having asserted that any ornament ought to be obliged to serve a structural necessity. Wright also discerned patterns and textures in nature that often approached the abstract. In stone he found the basic grammar of the earth. When he conceived stone walls as the abstraction of native rock structure, they seemed already caressed and blessed by the ages [54]. He thought wood to be the most intimate and kind of all materials, far too beautiful to be painted; it was better stained or left to weather a silver gray, like the branches and bark of trees [55]. Long, thin courses of brick quickened to the rhythm of the prairie [56]. Through time, and with decay, a wall of common brick could turn as softly radiant as an old tapestry [57]. Copper cornices changed to a rich verdigris. Steel, although lacking in texture or grain, offered great strength: It served quietly and surreptitiously, as the armature of a cantilever or as a spidery structural network. Reinforced concrete captured the imagination through its strength and especially its plastic character. It could be cast into continuously flowing surfaces and monolithic structure [58]. Glass was yet another story.

NATURE AND GLASS

Wright regarded glass as the materialization of light, the weightless medium of sight. He found it to be the most paradoxical material of architecture and the most complex in relation to nature. As a solid plane through which one could see with perfect clarity, glass opened a building to the landscape; it also acted as a lens by which the landscape could be structured with a grace sufficient to make pictorial art redundant [59]. Glass also served as an analogue to all the lakes and ponds that Thoreau took to be earth's eye on the sky; for it reflected the landscape with a luxuriance that shimmered with every breath of wind or change in light [60–62]. Glass could be as refractive as ice [63]. Or it could be composed of colored panes and of panes as iridescent as a butterfly's wings [64, 65].

Wright had good reasons, then, for choosing glass as the primary vehicle of his ornament. His glass designs were conceived purely within the grammar of geometry native to the drafting board. A glass pattern never should be confused with the landscape, he said, because the duty of architecture was to imitate nature at a much deeper level. Casement windows and glass doors provided clean planes for geometric design. The reflected landscape merely flickered on the surface in an insubstantial way, without destroying the integrity of the glass plane or its pattern. It was not Wright's way to plunder nature for ready-made forms; even his sumac patterns in the Dana house were vigorously abstract, and expressed other moments of

59. South bedroom window of the Hardy house, Racine, Wisconsin.

60. Prairie pond at evening.

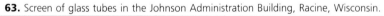

61. Bedroom casements of the Bradley house, Kankakee, Illinois.

63. Screen of glass tubes in the Johnson Administration Building, Racine, Wisconsin.

62. Living-room casement of the Tomek house, Riverside, Illinois.

64. Panes in a living-room casement of the Robie house, Chicago, Illinois.

65. Entrance of the Adams house, Oak Park, Illinois.

66. Breakfast nook of the Dana house, Springfield, Illinois.

67. Leaf from a river birch tree.

68. Budding lilacs.

69. Entrance of the Dana house, Springfield, Illinois.

70. Butterfly, Springfield, Illinois.

nature just as well [66–68]. The butterfly wreaths at the entrance likewise proved more richly suggestive than the butterfly in nature [69, 70]. Wright's inventive patterns with the metal cames, the flat bars which bonded the panes into place, may have been inspired by the dark veins in a butterfly's wings; but again his design looked more vital than that in the living creature [71, 72]. The glass design in the master bedroom ostensibly joined the sumac to the butterfly, yet it suggested, too, the wings of a hovering damselfly, which nature, to safeguard the creature, made transparent, to be less visible and to cast no shadow [73, 74].

71. Living room of the Dana house, Springfield, Illinois.

72. Butterfly, southern Wisconsin.

74. Damselfly.

73. Master bedroom of the Dana house, Springfield, Illinois.

FIELDS AS ORNAMENT

Flowers beyond number spotted the meadows of the prairie. Wright held fond memories of the fields from his youth. He soon saw broad wall surfaces as potential fields of ornamental pattern. In nature, fields were found in many ways. The leaves of a prairie redbud formed fields as lyrical as those of the water plants from which Wright abstracted one of his first window designs [75, 76]. A cherry tree blossomed against the sky much like the friezes that Wright designed for the Winslow and Dana houses [77, 78]. The lichens on a hawthorn were like his mosaics for the Coonley house [79, 80]. Yet these patterns soon disappeared from Wright's work. He moved on to a more basic discovery, that the elements of construction, whether stones or bricks or boards or patterned concrete blocks, created ornamental fields within the very structure of a building.

75. Redbud leaves.

76. Dining-room casements of Wright's home, Oak Park, Illinois.

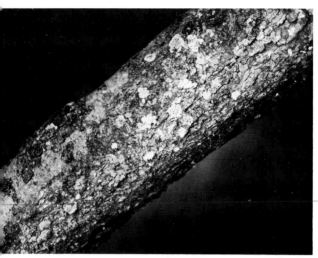

79. Lichens on a hawthorn limb.

77. Cherry tree in blossom.

78. Second-story frieze of the Dana house, Springfield, Illinois.

80. Tile patterns of the Coonley house, Riverside, Illinois.

LIKE A LIVING BEING

Louis Sullivan spoke of nature's eloquence of organization. The idea that a building might aspire to a level of organization as high as that of an organic being took hold in Wright's mind with great force. He saw that Sullivan's work often fell short, except in its flourishes of ornament, and he challenged himself to extend through the entire fabric of a building the fluency that Sullivan could command in his finest ornament. Nature invited imitation on various levels. Wright nearly always avoided the lowest level,

88. Project for the McCormick house, Lake Forest, Illinois.

89. Living room at Taliesin.

90. Crown of an oak tree.

THE NATURAL POETRY OF STRUCTURE

What reasonable man, asked Thoreau, could ever suppose that ornament in nature was something outward and merely of the skin? Wright meant to achieve a natural concordance between structure and ornament. If the plan was to be the most succinct and abstract presentation of the essential character and structure of a building, and if ornament represented the flowering of structure, then the plan itself should have an inherent pattern of mass, proportion and rhythm. The plan should be a work of art. It represented the way a building was to lie upon the land, taking the place of just that much of nature [91]. Wright said there ought to be more beauty in a plan than in almost any of its consequences [92]. A plan thus became ornamental, and an ornament might well look like a plan [93]. Sometimes an ornament would echo the elevation [94]. A small fixture could easily become as articulated as the plan of a major building [95, 96]. As his ornament grew more abstract and more nourished by his plans, Wright drew ever closer to the principles of form in nature [97]. To judge an architect, he said, one must look to the plan. A master showed his hand there or never.

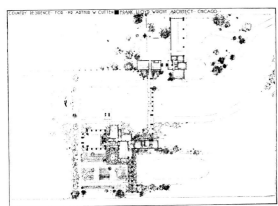

91. Project for the Cutten house, near Wheaton, Illinois.

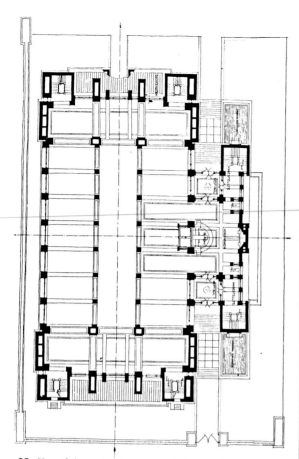

92. Plan of the Larkin Building, Buffalo, New York.

93. Casement in the studio of the Dana house,
Springfield, Illinois.

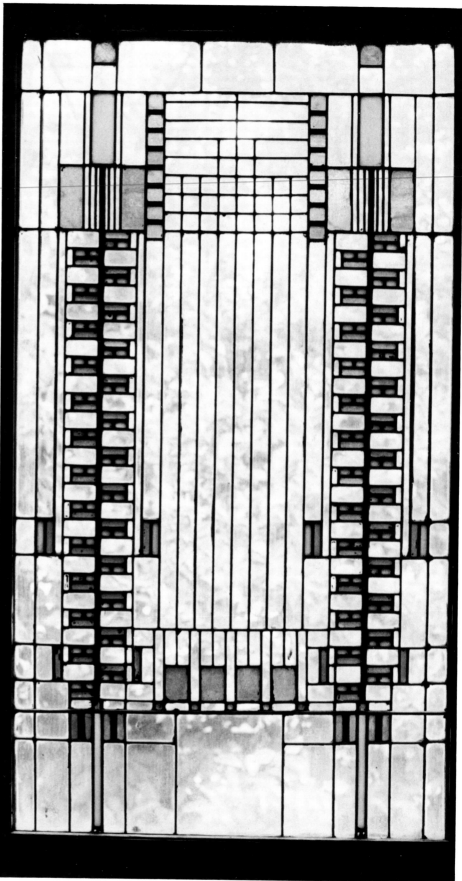

94. Living-room ceiling lights in the Heurtley house, Oak Park, Illinois.

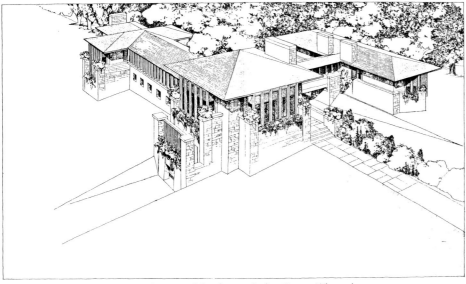

96. Hillside Home School, near Spring Green, Wisconsin.

95. Wall-mounted lamp in the Willits house, Highland Park, Illinois.

97. Casements in the Coonley house, Riverside, Illinois.

NATURE'S HIDDEN PLACES

Because the prairie was so exposed to the harsh forces of nature, it begged for secret and sheltering places. Hamlin Garland remembered the rains of springtime filling the ravines and adding a strangeness and dignity to the prairie; Wilhelm Miller, seeking to understand the Illinois landscape, identified many elements that functioned as a foil to the prairie, such as the woods and ravines, rocks and bluffs and riverbanks. In the same spirit, much about Wright's architecture was oblique and mysterious. Plans as different as those of the Heurtley house, the Robie house and Unity Temple shared the odd characteristic that in each the path to the principal interior space required seven right-angle turns. Or the access might be delayed by a series of forecourts [98–100]. Wright's entrances often echoed the fruit cellars and storm shelters of folk tradition, for almost always they were small and deeply shadowed [101, 102].

Jens Jensen spoke of wandering along a rippling brook to a shadowy cove where every nook was drenched in the mysticism of the forest; the architect R. M. Schindler said that he found free nature flowing through Wright's houses as in a forest. Floor levels changed and directions changed; to form the reality of interior space, shadow became almost as important as light. Shadow and light were finally conjoined at the hearth, where Wright took great comfort in watching a fire deep within the masonry of a building. He wrote of the fireplaces at Taliesin as primeval openings that sent streams of light and warmth into his home [103].

98. Work court at Taliesin.

99. Midway court at Taliesin.

100. Entrance to the forecourt at Taliesin.

101. Entrance to the Tomek house, Riverside, Illinois.

102. Entrance to the Thomas house, Oak Park, Illinois.

103. Living-room fireplace at Taliesin.

FOREST LIGHT

104. Illinois woodland, as formed by Jens Jensen at the Lincoln Memorial Garden, Lake Springfield.

Jens Jensen planted trees in ways that created soft transitions from shadow into sunlight [104]. When he built his last home, he called it The Clearing, because he believed forest clearings or sun openings were symbolic of a clearing of the mind. Wright shared many of his values and, whenever possible, oriented a building to the south or southeast and opened the principal rooms through long ranges of windows or glass doors, as clearings for light and air and vistas [105, 106]. At the same time, the extremes of the prairie climate had led him to seek an umbrageous architecture. Ceilings thus became a metaphor of the forest cover, quietly sheltering the life below in friendship. Robert C. Spencer, jr., noted that the high and patterned windows of Wright's library in the Oak Park studio were conceived as a tracery of leaves against the sky. In the Bradley house, a few years later, it was easy to see in the glass designs an abstraction of flowers rising beneath the branches of the ceiling [107]. Wright was trying to bring wall and ceiling together, to form a unified interior and a more complete analogue of the outdoors [108]. Lingering traces of beams or joists soon gave way to more fantastic patterns, suggesting the pitched planes of the roof [109]. Wright began to merge the planes of the ceiling and walls through panels of different colors, or with long strips of wood that he variously called rib-bands, wood-bands, marking-bands, marking-strips, plastic ribbons or simply wood strip. He used them to make the ceiling come down into the wall, and, conversely, to make the room rise generously into what appeared to be the reaches of the roof [110, 111]. Finally, he achieved the tranquillity of an umbrageous architecture even without the strips [112].

Ceilings also served as a source of forest light, the equivalent of what Emerson had called the tempered light of the woods. Wright from the beginning was preoccupied with light from above. In 1893, he said, he had begun to experiment with diffused light in the anteroom of his Chicago office by dropping a ceiling of patterned glass to the height of the doors; the effect of lights from above it was like sunlight. He thought that rays of sunlight stood for joy, the essential truth to be set against the pain of the world, and that an awareness of the sky ought to be as much a part of daily indoor life as an awareness of the earth. His son John was pleased to remember from the Oak Park years the light that filtered through fret-sawed ceiling grilles [113]. The arabesque of the dining-room panel was bordered in oak-leaf patterns, and the panels of the playroom ceiling were based on sprays of prickly ash. Wright soon conceived much more abstract designs, however, as analogues to what he spoke of as mosaics of foliage in the sun. If the ceiling lights of Unity Temple were meant to cast a warm glow like sunlight, the side-aisle lights of the Robie house, patterned with squared oak

105. South aisle of the Tomek house, Riverside, Illinois.

106. Living room at Taliesin.

107. Living room of the Bradley house, Kankakee, Illinois.

108. Dining-room ceiling in the Willits house, Highland Park, Illinois.

109. Living-room ceiling in the Heurtley house, Oak Park, Illinois.

110. Unity Temple, Oak Park, Illinois.

112. Ceiling at Wingspread, north of Racine, Wisconsin.

111. Ceiling of the Hardy house, Racine, Wisconsin.

113. Dining room of Wright's home, Oak Park, Illinois.

114. Ceiling lights in Unity Temple, Oak Park, Illinois.

sticks and accent blocks, served better at night, like moonlight [114, 115]. Forest openings could also be suggested by high sources of light in unexpected places [116].

Wright described the large drafting room at Taliesin as an abstract forest with light streaming through an interwoven pattern of wood trusses. He was also happy with light filtered by overhead panels of canvas, first at his temporary desert camp and then at Taliesin West. The clerestory lights in the Johnson house, north of Racine, were much like openings in a leafy cover [117]. The main workspace of the Johnson Administration Building, a forest of concrete columns, gained its light from clusters of glass tubes in the ceiling [118, 119]. Wright conceived the Guggenheim Museum as a lighting project, a courting of the sun [120]. Of one of his last designs, the project for an Arizona capitol, he said that the sheltering canopy would be like a great tree, filtering the sunlight.

When he thought back to the days of his youth, Wright wrote of the sunlight slanting through the trees and falling on leaf-covered ground. He understood the forest floor as a reflection of the forest ceiling, and from the light that danced on the ground—the "flakes of sunshine," as Ruskin called them—he drew his feeling for the play of sun splashes on the floor of a building [121]. His patterns in rugs and table scarves and doorway curtains were meant to work with the sunlight in creating forest harmonies [122].

115. Aisle soffit light of the Robie house, Chicago, Illinois.

116. Living room at
Taliesin.

117. Central space at Wingspread, north of Racine, Wisconsin.

118. Johnson Administration Building, Racine, Wisconsin.

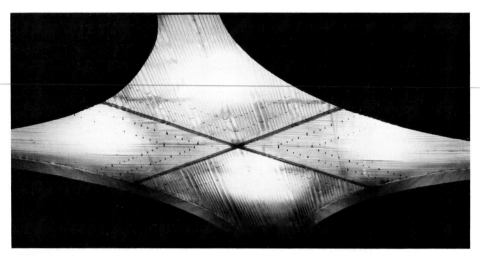

119. Ceiling lights in the Johnson Administration Building, Racine, Wisconsin.

120. Guggenheim Museum, New York.

121. Hollyhock House, Hollywood, Los Angeles, California.

122. Living room of the Coonley house, Riverside, Illinois.

The ceiling came down into the walls, and the walls grew directly into the fixtures and furniture. Every detail belonged to the body of the building. Wright liked walls of undisguised plaster, wood, brick, stone or glass—all materials directly expressive of their strength and character [123]. He detested paint and wallpaper, for they were masks. Thoreau, at springtime thaw, studied the patterns in a bank of sand and reported that he had stood in the laboratory of the creator; he delighted also in burning river shells to make the lime for plastering his cabin. Wright cherished the sand-finish plaster surfaces at Taliesin because they reminded him of the flat stretches of the river below, from which the sand indeed had come. He enriched some of the surfaces with gold leaf, but typically gave the plaster walls of his buildings a scumbled look, heavily textured and saturated with complex colors that suggested the passage of much time [124, 125].

Ruskin wrote that an architect should look to nature for the management of color just as for the development of form; the true colors of architecture, he said, were those to be found in stone. Wright said to go to the

123. Living-room alcove at Taliesin.

124. Gold leaf on a wall at Taliesin.

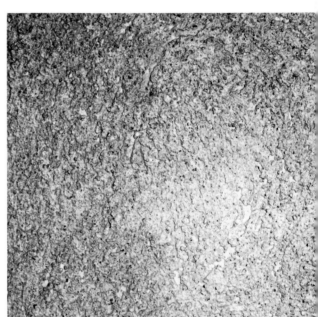

125. Wall surface in the Tomek house, Riverside, Illinois.

126. Wall-mounted lamp in the Dana house, Springfield, Illinois.

127. Summer sky, west of Oak Park, Illinois.

woods and fields for color schemes, and to choose the soft, warm, op-
timistic tones of earths and autumn leaves: golden browns and olive greens
and the tans and reds of soil. The color of wood figured large in most of his
harmonies because the furniture usually was made from the same wood as
the doors and trim and marking-bands. Each piece, whether freestanding or
casework, became an active extension of the basic character of the building.
Wright loved the colors and markings of wood. He preferred straight and
thin grains for longer members and, for wide panels, grains figured like
waves. In fixtures he sometimes used panes of iridescent glass in colors like
those of the evening sky or of reflections in summer ponds [126, 127].

SMALL-SCALE SYMMETRIES

Nature finds perfect satisfaction in radial or bilateral symmetries at small scale. Small organisms often assume the stricter symmetries that would be tedious at larger scale and not convincing expressions of more complex functions [128, 129]. So there are many instances when nature may be compared with the rotated and radial symmetries of Wright's fixtures [130–132]. Bilateral symmetry, like that of a milkweed pod spread open to scatter its seeds, served at slightly larger scale [133, 134]. Ruskin said that the mightiest type of form ever conceived by the mind of man was based exclusively on associations of the circle and square. In those most regular of figures, Wright also found great power; he formed his personal sign from a circle within a quartered square. Later, by 1900, he changed it to a simple red square. Yet the earlier design appeared again in such details as the ceiling lamps of the Robie house, which glowed like suns over quarter-sections of farmland [135].

128. Dandelion with spider.

129. Rose.

130. Ceiling lamp in the Dana house, Springfield, Illinois.

131. Two gourds.

132. Table lamp in the Dana house, Springfield, Illinois.

133. Milkweed pod.

134. Bathroom casement in the Robie house, Chicago, Illinois.

135. Ceiling lamp in the Robie house, Chicago, Illinois.

NATURE RETRIEVED

Carried indoors, souvenirs of nature served as special correspondents with the open air [136–138]. Wright favored leafy branches, ferns, weeds and wildflowers. Living creatures such as these spoke no language, William C. Gannett had written in his tract *The House Beautiful*, but, like children, rewarded love with an answering loveliness. Gannett praised the faculty for transferring nature indoors; he mentioned mosses, ferns and dried leaves as good candidates. Wright furnished his home in Oak Park with elegant copper vessels designed to display such fragments of nature. Wildflowers and weeds thus became icons of the prairie, while branches and ferns spoke of the woods.

136. Morning at Taliesin, with fresh-cut sprays.

137. Dried flowers and weeds in the Tomek house, Riverside, Illinois.

138. Ferns near Taliesin.

FRIENDS OF NATURE

Wright respected all those who had honored nature before him, and particularly the first Americans and the traditional Japanese. By 1890, when the frontier was declared closed, the Indian had been so utterly subdued that he had been forced into his place in myth. Wright embraced the romantic image of the Indian as a man of strength and cunning, wise especially in the ways of nature. He stood statuettes of Indians by Hermon MacNeil at the door to his first office, in downtown Chicago, and he placed the same artist's *Primitive Chant* near the inglenook of the Winslow house in suburban River Forest, his first major work. The same piece appeared in a rendering of the Dana house library, along with an inset panel of ornament based on arrows; arrows also formed the finials on the master-bedroom dressers [139, 140]. For his own master bedroom in Oak Park, he asked Orlando Giannini to paint murals of an Indian chief and squaw. He may well have thought of himself every time he looked at the chief, said John Lloyd Wright, because in later years, on a stone outcropping from which he would overlook Taliesin, he habitually struck the same pose. In 1924 Erich Mendelsohn found Wright dressed for hiking in a fantastic Indian garment complete with bark shoes and tomahawk. The same year, Wright conceived two Indian sculptures as memorials to the Winnebagos, once the lords over most of Wisconsin [141].

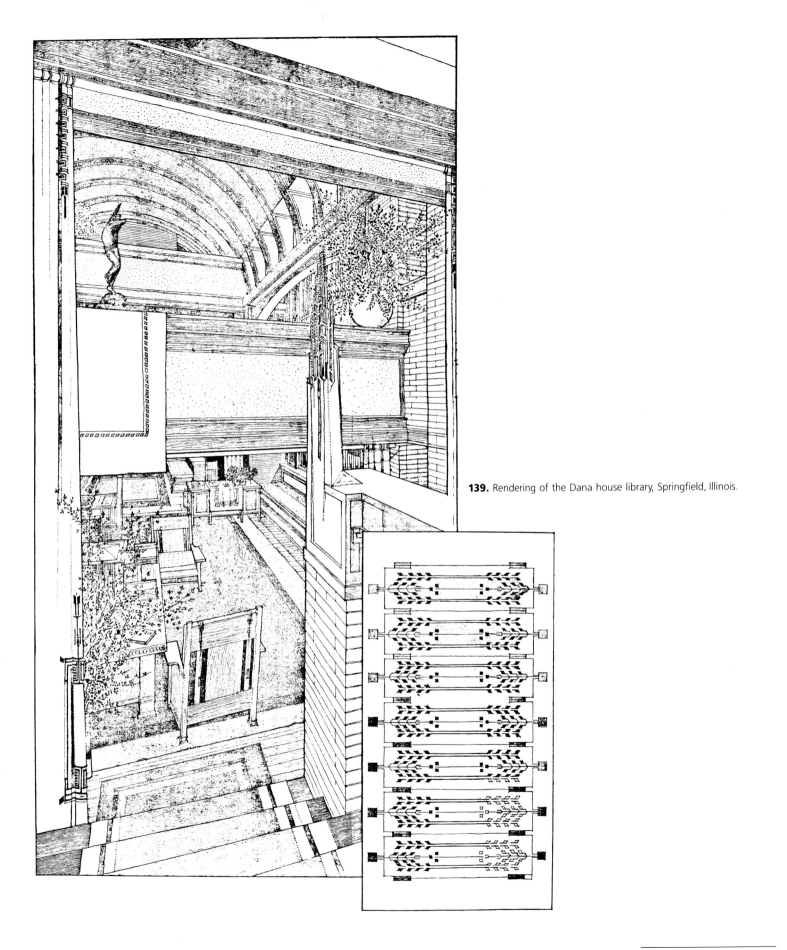

139. Rendering of the Dana house library, Springfield, Illinois.

140. Finial of a dresser in the Dana house, Springfield, Illinois.

141. *Nakoma, Warrior*, at the Hillside Home School, near Spring Green, Wisconsin.

Wright echoed the feathers of an arrow in the glass pattern of the Steffens house and in details of the Robie house [142]. He said Aline Barnsdall was as near American as any Indian, and in the abstract relief he designed for the mantel of her living-room fireplace in the Hollyhock House he portrayed her as an Indian princess surveying her lands. He wrote that friendly Indians still lingered in the valley of the Wisconsin River when his ancestors settled there and, from his autumn days on the farm, he recalled the wigwam rows of corn shocks. He named one of his Lake Tahoe cabin designs the wigwam type; he described his project for the Nakoma Country Club, in Madison, Wisconsin, as an Indianesque affair; and he referred to the main space of the Johnson house as a high wigwam.

Wright's allusions to Indians were accents in building environments

142. Wall-mounted lamp in the Robie house, Chicago, Illinois.

dedicated to the native soil. His highest tribute perhaps was to be found in the attention he paid to fireplaces, for Indians and fires were inseparable; the Indians of southern Michigan in fact used the same word for fire as for prairie. In the same spirit, Jens Jensen fashioned stone council rings as a basic element of his landscape art; at the Lincoln Memorial Garden, his extraordinarily understated composition by the shores of Lake Springfield, in central Illinois, a series of eight council rings formed the only salient feature. Jensen intended the council rings to harbor the prairie fire and promote a spirit of democratic equality among all those who sat around them. Wright regarded the hearth as an Indian campfire taken indoors [143]. He specified a campfire in the center of the main wigwam of the Nakoma Country Club, and he had an indoor campfire at the center of his Ocatillo Desert Camp in Arizona.

143. Fireplace at Wingspread, north of Racine, Wisconsin.

144. The Wisconsin River near Taliesin.

Wright came to admire traditional Japanese domestic architecture naturally enough, because so much about the prairie suggested an Oriental sensibility: the splendor of the grasses, the mists above the rivers or summer morning fields, the beautiful structure of the wood barns [144, 145]. Spencer wrote that nature was the source to which Wright always turned for inspiration, and if not to nature at first hand, then to its great interpreters, the Orientals and especially the Japanese. Wright wanted to learn what nature worship might mean for an indigenous architecture. He said that Japanese art knew the school of nature more intimately than that of any other people; it expressed nature in simple and spontaneous ways and unerringly discovered geometric equivalents to the form characteristics of nature's creations. Japanese prints, he thought, were the most exquisite graphic art of all time. He often followed the same ideals in his own presentation drawings. He loved the mellow texture of rice paper and the deep patina of bronze, and he believed that the Japanese had understood the nature of wood better than anyone else. He admired their standards of clean workmanship. From the traditional Japanese house, which he considered masterly, he refined his own style of displaying weeds and flowers and branches. He also paid great

145. Damaged barn in southern Iowa.

attention to niches and inglenooks, which could serve like the *tokonoma*. Japanese architecture encouraged him in opening the walls of his buildings into screens for light and air, and in reducing the separation of rooms and the amount of furniture in them. His love of wood and his design of fixtures often spoke of his sympathy for Japanese ideals [146]. He used wood screens to divide space more subtly than walls could. Much as the Japanese had used the *tatami* mat as a module for the floor plan, Wright used a module to maintain a strong sense of order and human scale in even the most occult of his plans. The sweep of his roofs, their deep eaves and their elaborate cornices easily found companionship in the old buildings of Japan [147].

146. Suspended lamps in Unity Temple, Oak Park, Illinois.

147. Cornice detail of the Dana house, Springfield, Illinois.

NATURE AND TIME

Jens Jensen wrote of a prairie cottonwood so large that its first branch came seventy-five feet above the ground; when the tree was cut down, it was found to be more than six hundred years old. Ruskin said that a building could not be considered to have reached its prime until four or five centuries had passed over it. Wright could see that nature everywhere marked the passage of time, that the destiny of a tiny seedling was to age into a great tree [148]. He chose the materials of his buildings to receive the slow blessings of nature and to speak about time [149, 150]. A house of true character, he said, stood a good chance of growing more valuable with age. His home in Wisconsin looked as if it had been there for centuries, and his winter home in Arizona seemed not so much constructed as excavated. Organic change not only was inevitable, he wrote, but a good friend [151]. A natural architecture, through time, would be enriched by nature [152].

148. Oak seedling.

149. Rock ledge in northern Illinois.

150. Stone wall of the Hillside Home School, near Spring Green, Wisconsin.

151. Fallen redbud leaves.

152. South fixed light in the Robie House, Chicago, Illinois.

We can sense in Wright's buildings that he had tapped into some great source, and we find the pages of his autobiography filled with the most lyrical images of nature, often as he reconstructs them in the mind of a wondering child. Wright was careless of facts but not about the depth of his relation to nature, and the central theme of his life's story is much the same as in Whitman's poem:

> There was a child went forth every day,
> And the first object he look'd upon, that object he became,
> And that object became part of him for the day or a certain part of the day,
> Or for many years or stretching cycles of years,
> The early lilacs became part of this child,
> And grass and white and red morning-glories. . . .

As a young architect he often rode his horse out onto the prairie to gather weeds for his special copper vases and urns. He photographed them, and published some of these tender pictures in his printing of *The House Beautiful*, ornamented also with his intricate graphic patterns. "With nature-warp of naked weed by printer-craft imprisoned," he wrote, "we weave this interlinear web." Thirty years later, he began writing his autobiography by recalling the play of naked weed against the snow. Weeds furnished splendid models of nature's endless patterns in structure. They flourished on the prairie, where freedom spoke louder, said Jens Jensen, than anywhere else in the world. They found kinship with such of Whitman's verses as "I

153. Cherry tree, leafing.

154. Trees at Taliesin.

announce natural persons to arise" or "I announce the great individual, fluid as Nature, chaste, affectionate, compassionate, fully arm'd." Louis Sullivan also was to make much of weeds in his *Kindergarten Chats*; but it was an earlier essay of Sullivan's, from 1894, the very year that Wright claimed to have set down his own philosophy, that more fully suggested what Wright meant to be about.

Almost in the same breath, Sullivan expressed dismay "that man, Nature's highest product, should alone have gone awry," and yet forecast "the richness, fullness and variety that might and should come from the man's brain with the impulse of nature's fecundity flowing through it." Man's fall from grace is equivalent, then, to his disharmony with nature. The architect, as a man, belongs to the family of nature's highest creatures. If he chooses to "meet modern discoveries, calibers, nature face to face"—Whitman once more, in words that Wright chose for his *Architectural Forum* portfolio of 1938—man can grow to serve as nature's instrument. If nature can be seen as a metaphor of architecture, then architecture can become a metaphor of nature. And so Wright was satisfied to take his diploma from nature. "Nature is loved by what is best in us," Emerson had said; and Ruskin wrote that "the disciplined eye and the life in the woods are worth more than all botanical knowledge"; Whitman sang of the open air and of the freedom to "no longer take things at second or third hand, nor / look

155. Roadside flower, near Taliesin.

through the eyes of the dead, nor feed on the / spectres in books," and Sullivan said that it was education's greatest crime to have removed men from nature.

Nature offered the moral corrective to the debased life of the modern city, a dreary, confused, sterile, ugly, unhealthy place. "Cities give not the human senses room enough," said Emerson. Thoreau worried even about village life. "We need the tonic of wildness," he said. Ruskin wrote that the advantage of living in a city was counterbalanced by the loss of friendship with nature, that the true function of architecture was to tell men about nature. In such a spirit, Wright made his city buildings more intense and

156. Prairie roses, northern Iowa.

self-enclosed; he wanted them to take the place of a lost nature, to make reparation for their dismal sites, which he described as barren town lots devoid of tree or natural incident. Sullivan wrote that all great ideas and impulses were born in the open air, close to nature; he said the lake and the prairie were emblems of pride, fertility, power and graciousness, which encircled and enfolded the city "as a wistful mother holds a subnormal child." Wright remembered Sullivan as having produced his esoteric and efflorescent ornament in the poetry-crushing environment of a more cruel materialism than any seen since the days of ancient Rome. Chicago was the type of city that had moved Ruskin to say that everything was being manufactured except men, for the division of labor was in fact a division of men into small crumbs of life.

Nature sustained Wright's manliness in architecture, that quality which set his work apart from the canons of Arts and Crafts taste, so pallid and polite. The difference was virtually one of gender. Charles E. White, jr., busy in Wright's studio with the working drawings for Unity Temple in 1906, predicted that the building would be widely criticized, but would live on. "It has a virile quality that cannot die," he wrote. Wright had learned from nature to keep his strokes as clean and uncompromised as he could make them.

At the same time, nature guided Wright toward the generous, the luxuriant. Emerson observed the profusion and prodigality of nature, and declared exaggeration to be in the course of things; Ruskin praised the exuberance of the Gothic, because no architecture was so haughty, he said, as that which disdained "either by the complexity or the attractiveness of its features, to embarrass our investigation, or betray us into delight." Thoreau gave thanks for the wild luxuries of nature, and said his inheritance was not narrow. That nature could tolerate man, wrote Sullivan, was further evi-

157. Prairie plants, northern Iowa.

158. Taliesin landscape.

dence of her bounty. Wright came of age on the Illinois prairie, the most fertile land in all the world. The springs of inspiration could never run dry, he said, for the human spirit in love with nature's exuberance [153]. Nature expressed itself through the elemental poetry of all its structure, which was the source of all abstraction. Every true aesthetic, he said, was an implication of nature, because in nature lay the fountainhead of all forms whatsoever.

Nature not only was the source, but the standard. If nature meant the principle that gave life its form and character, then architecture ought to be seen as nature-pattern, it ought to have the countenance of a completely organized being [154]. Through a sympathy for nature's ways, Wright said, the indigenous architectures of the world had spoken of the love of life which quietly and inevitably finds the right way, as little concerned with literature as the flower by the wayside is concerned with the farmer who

159. Taliesin.

passes in the road [155]. Nature offered the only true guide to scale, proportions and the right relation between whole and parts. Wright wanted his designs to grow as though plants, for nature had style and was beyond fashion [156]. Style resided not in a fixed form, Viollet-le-Duc had written in the sixth of his discourses, but in the true expression of a principle; and because nothing existed in nature without a principle, everything in nature had to have style. Thus the named styles in architecture suggested only dead formulas, or, at best, principles that were no longer operative in modern life.

Wilhelm Miller, at the end of his essay on *The Prairie Spirit in Landscape Gardening*, noted that his illustrations had included houses by Sullivan, Spencer, William Drummond and Wright; and noted also that Wright had declined to give or recognize any name for this work. Wright in fact had chided Miller for the academic habit of refusing to recognize a creative individual until his work was absorbed by that of a group or sect. The very idea of a prairie style, or prairie school, suggested the second-rate. Wright was after style in the generic sense. Emerson had said that character was nature in the highest form. Charles E. White, jr., wrote from Oak Park in 1903 that Wright had told him to stop reading and to do nothing but study nature: "He says to continually and eternally sketch the forms of trees—'a man who can sketch from memory the different trees, with their characteristics faithfully portrayed, will be a good architect'!"

Nature was the model for style; style was the poetic manifestation of character; and the true property of character was individuality. "Each individual plant," Jens Jensen said, "has a song to sing, a story to tell" [157]. Emerson said that nature never rhymed her children, nor made two men alike. If the purpose of architecture is to present man, said Wright, then all buildings should serve to liberate the lives of individuals, all houses should take on the character of the individual with perpetual and bewildering variety. Emerson, Thoreau and Whitman all stood behind Wright when he said that he wished to build for the illustrious sovereignty of the individual. The best part of beauty, Emerson said, was the radiation of human character from the work of art, such character that one was reminded of nothing else, because it took the place of the whole creation. Ruskin had written that individualism belonged especially to northerners, which meant that the most noble Gothic architecture, although Catholic, was nevertheless essentially protestant in spirit; and Wright took great pride in calling Taliesin a house of the north. By sanctioning individuality, nature encouraged an architecture of romance and mystery. Romance, said Wright, was the operation of freedom in creating form controlled only by the sense of proportion; the mysterious was that which emanated from a whole so organic as to have lost all sign of how it was made.

Emerson called nature the most ancient religion. He said the mind loved its old home. Thoreau found nature to be the one perennial source. And so did Sullivan; that is why Wright venerated him, although his own architecture went far past Sullivan's in its abstraction, its feeling for space, its sympathy for materials and its grasp of the cantilever, in place of the arch, as the most liberating of all structural principles. Nature was not easy to read, Wright said, but was inexhaustible. Nothing could be found in nature that was not sacred. The infinite attention that nature paid to individuality revealed that both spoke of the divinity. Nature study was the only source for a sound philosophy upon which to base a new aesthetic [158].

Man, the high creature of nature, held the potential for serving as one of nature's instruments in asserting the principle of life. A true work of art, Wright said, embodied the life spirit, and the true architect possessed the faculty of getting himself born into whatever he did, and born again and again, in fresh patterns, as new problems arose. Architecture was the opportunity to make man's reflection in his environment a godlike thing. Its aim could be nothing less than the creation of man as a perfect follower of nature. By choosing to meet nature face to face, an architect could make ready to embark on the greatest of all excursions [159].

ACKNOWLEDGMENTS AND SOURCES

To those who have made possible my visits to Wright's buildings and who have otherwise encouraged this study, I remain very grateful: Robert Kostka, Donald P. Hallmark, Maya Moran, Jack Prost, Sakip Altay, J. and M. Yoghourtjian, Jean P. Murphy, Donald Kalec, Mark Heyman, Peter Kountz, Mrs. Frank Lloyd Wright, Bruce Brooks Pfeiffer, William Wesley Peters, Susan and Kenn Lockhart, Charles and Minerva Montooth and Vina Jacobs.

When the text was threatened by hundreds of footnotes, I decided they were better left silent; but the written sources that I have turned to are these:

Angle, Paul M., ed., *Prairie State: Impressions of Illinois, 1673–1967* (Chicago, 1968).

Broun, Elizabeth, "American Paintings and Sculpture in the Fine Arts Building of the World's Columbian Exposition, Chicago, 1893," Ph.D. diss., the University of Kansas, 1976.

Caldwell, Alfred, "Jens Jensen: the Prairie Spirit," *Landscape Architecture* LI (Jan. 1961), 102–105.

Christy, Stephen F., "The Prairie Spirit," in *An Open Land: Photographs of the Midwest, 1852–1982*, ed. Victoria Post Ranney (Chicago, 1983).

Craven, Wayne, *Sculpture in America* (New York, 1968).

Eaton, Leonard K., *Landscape Artist in America: The Life and Work of Jens Jensen* (Chicago, 1964).

Emerson, Ralph Waldo, *Essays*, intro. by Irwin Edman (New York, 1926).

Garland, Hamlin, *Boy Life on the Prairie* (New York, 1899).

Jensen, Jens, *Siftings* (Chicago, 1939).

———. *The Clearing* (Chicago, 1949).

———, "Some Gardens of the Middle West," *Architectural Review* XV (May 1908), 93–95.

———, "An Open-Air Exhibition of American Sculpture," *Architectural Review* XVI (May 1909), 57–59.

Kahlenberg, Mary Hunt, and Mark Schwartz, *A Book About Grass* (New York, 1983).

Madson, John, *Where the Sky Began* (Boston, 1982).

McCoy, Esther, *Vienna to Los Angeles: Two Journeys* (Santa Monica, Calif. 1979).

Mendelsohn, Eric, *Letters of an Architect*, ed. Oskar Beyer (London, 1967).

Mies van der Rohe, Ludwig, "A Tribute to Frank Lloyd Wright," *College Art Journal* VI (Autumn 1946), 41–42.

Miller, Wilhelm, *The Prairie Spirit in Landscape Gardening* (Urbana, Ill., 1915).

Moran, Maya, "In the Garden With Frank Lloyd Wright," *Inland Architect* 28 (March–April 1984), 26–29.

Morris, Alfred, "A Consistent Home," *Sketch Book* V (Sept. 1905), 20.

Morse, Edward S., *Japanese Homes and Their Surroundings* (Boston, 1886; Dover reprint, 1961).

Moser, Werner M., *Frank Lloyd Wright: Sixty Years of Living Architecture* (Winterthur, Switz., 1952).

Pfeiffer, Bruce Brooks, *Frank Lloyd Wright Drawings from 1893–1959* (New York, 1983).

———, *Indian Memorials* ([?], 1974).

Ruskin, John, *Modern Painters*, vol. II (London, 1846).

———, *The Seven Lamps of Architecture* (London, 1849).

———, *The Stones of Venice* (London, 1851–1853).

———, *The Elements of Drawing* (London, 1857; Dover reprint, 1971).

Sandburg, Carl, *Complete Poems* (New York, 1950).

Sell, Henry Blackman, "Interpretation not Imitation," *International Studio* LV (1915), lxxix–lxxxii.

Smith, Kathryn, "Frank Lloyd Wright, Hollyhock House, and Olive Hill, 1914–1924," *Journal of the Society of Architectural Historians* XXXVIII (March 1979), 15–33.

Smith, Nancy K. Morris, "Letters, 1903–1906, by Charles E. White, Jr., from the Studio of Frank Lloyd Wright," *Journal of Architectural Education* XXV (Fall 1971), 104–112.

Spencer, Robert C., jr., "The Work of Frank Lloyd Wright," *Architectural Review* XII (June 1900), 61–72.

Sullivan, Louis H., *Kindergarten Chats and Other Writings* (New York, 1947; Dover reprint, 1979).

Tafel, Edgar, *Apprentice to Genius* (New York, 1979; Dover reprint as *Years with Frank Lloyd Wright: Apprentice to Genius*, 1985).

Tallmadge, Thomas E., "The 'Chicago School,'" *Architectural Review* XV (April 1908), 69–74.

———, *The Story of Architecture in America*, rev. ed. (New York, 1936).

Thompson, D'Arcy Wentworth, *On Growth and Form*, 2nd ed. (Cambridge, England, 1942).

Thoreau, Henry David, *Walden and Other Writings*, ed. Joseph Wood Krutch (New York, 1962).

Tributsch, Helmut, *How Life Learned to Live* (Cambridge, Mass., 1982).

Viollet-le-Duc, E. E., *Discourses on Architecture*, trans. Henry Van Brunt (Boston, 1875).

Von Holst, Hermann Valentin, *Modern American Homes* (Chicago, 1913; Dover reprint as *Country and Suburban Homes of the Prairie School Period*, 1982).

Whitman, Walt, *Leaves of Grass*, ed. Lawrence Clark Powell (New York, 1964).

Wright, Frank Lloyd, "A Home in a Prairie Town," *Ladies' Home Journal* XVIII (Feb. 1901), 17.

———, "A Small House with 'Lots of Room in It,'" *Ladies' Home Journal* XVIII (July 1901), 15.

———, "A Fireproof House for $5,000," *Ladies' Home Journal* XXIV (April 1907), 24.

———, *Essays for the* Architectural Record *1908–1952* (New York, 1975).

———, *Ausgeführte Bauten und Entwürfe* (Berlin, 1910; Dover reprint as *Drawings and Plans of Frank Lloyd Wright: The Early Period (1893–1909)*, 1983).

———, *The Life-Work of the American Architect Frank Lloyd Wright*, ed., H. Th. Wijdeveld (Santpoort, Holland, 1925).

———, *Modern Architecture* (Princeton, N.J., 1931).

———, "Frank Lloyd Wright," *Architectural Forum* 68 (Jan. 1938), 1–102.

———, *An Organic Architecture* (London, 1939).

———, *On Architecture*, ed. Frederick Gutheim (New York, 1941).

———, *An Autobiography*, rev. ed. (New York, 1943).

———, *Genius and the Mobocracy* (New York, 1949).

———, *A Testament* (New York, 1957).

———, *Letters to Apprentices*, ed. Bruce Brooks Pfeiffer (Fresno, Calif., 1982).

———, *Letters to Architects*, ed. Bruce Brooks Pfeiffer (Fresno, Calif., 1984).

Wright, Gwendolyn, *Building the Dream: A Social History of Housing in America* (Cambridge, Mass., 1981).

Wright, John Lloyd, *My Father Who Is on Earth* (New York, 1946).

———, "Appreciation of Frank Lloyd Wright," *Architectural Design* XXX (Jan. 1960). opp. 3.

Wright, Olgivanna Lloyd, *Frank Lloyd Wright* (New York, 1966).

ALPHABETICAL LIST OF COMPLETED WRIGHT BUILDINGS
Mentioned in the Text, with Locations and Approximate Dates

Allen house, Wichita, Kansas, 1917
Adams house, Oak Park, Illinois, 1913–14
Bach house, Chicago, Illinois, 1915
Bradley house, Kankakee, Illinois, 1900
Cheney house, Oak Park, Illinois, 1903–04
Coonley house, Riverside, Illinois, 1908–11
Dana house, Springfield, Illinois, 1901–04
Fallingwater: *see* Kaufmann house
Guggenheim Museum, New York, New York, 1943–59
Hardy house, Racine, Wisconsin, 1905
Heurtley house, Oak Park, Illinois, 1902
Hills house, Oak Park, Illinois, 1906
Hillside Home School, near Spring Green, Wisconsin, 1901–03
Hollyhock house, Hollywood, Los Angeles, California, 1915–21
Imperial Hotel, Tokyo, Japan, 1913–23
Ingalls house, River Forest, Illinois, 1909
Johnson Administration Building, Racine, Wisconsin, 1936–39
Johnson house: *see* Wingspread
Kaufmann house (Fallingwater), near Mill Run, Pennsylvania, 1935–37
Larkin Building, Buffalo, New York, 1903–06
Martin (W. E.) house, Oak Park, Illinois, 1902–03
Midway Gardens, Chicago, Illinois, 1913–14
Ocatillo Desert Camp, Chandler, Arizona, 1928
Robie house, Chicago, Illinois, 1908–10
Steffens house, Chicago, Illinois, 1909
Taliesin, near Spring Green, Wisconsin, 1911 *ff.*
Taliesin West, Scottsdale, Arizona, 1938 *ff.*
Thomas house, Oak Park, Illinois, 1901–02
Tomek house, Riverside, Illinois, 1907–08
Unity Temple, Oak Park, Illinois, 1905–09
Westcott house, Springfield, Ohio, 1904
Willits house, Highland Park, Illinois, 1902–03
Wingspread, north of Racine, Wisconsin, 1937–38
Winslow house, River Forest, Illinois, 1893–94
Wright house and studio, Oak Park, Illinois, 1889–90; 1895–98